still
life

poems by
michael r guerin

Other Titles by Michael R. Guerin

POETRY:
Ghosts, Flames & Ashes
world thru a window
mind & machine
between black & white
still life
Found & Lost
beneath the waves
Flowers for Rumi
Ocean Rain
Vespers

FICTION:
The Otherside

ORACLE DECKS & GUIDEBOOKS:
Nature Speaks: A Lenormand Deck & Guidebook
Vincent Speaks: A Healing Oracle Deck & Guidebook

ISBN: 978-0-578-54225-6
Imprint: Independently published

Table of Contents

i. places

ii. things

"When one looks at one's own life, the everyday life that one lives and leads, it is so shallow, a verbal acceptance without any depth, a verbal explanation with which we seem to be so satisfied, a life that is so broken up..."

– J Krishnamurti

i. places

sunflowers (i)

the setting sun peeks
beneath a line of clouds
and casts long shadows
over peopled fields of sunflowers
standing ram-rod straight
stretching out to horizon's edge
in row upon row upon row...
their thick stalks bearing the weight
of heavy heads bowed low
with seed as they wait
patiently to release
their load.

bus stop

broken glass.
gum wrapper.
empty snapple bottle.
curiously, grains of sand
reminiscent
of the beach.

cars speed past
without a glance
in my direction
as i lean into the street
and look left
for a late
number seven bus.

up ahead, a faded fedora
shades an old man's
worn and weathered face
and fractured smile
which bobs
step by step
until he reaches
the rusted bench
and takes a seat.

dusk in voronezh

from an open
third floor balcony window

the deserted city square
still wet from afternoon rain

glistens in the glow
of four street lights below.

draped in a woolen shawl
her bare thighs exposed

to the cold
she sits lost in thought

gazing far out over
the sculptured horizon

as a delivery van rumbles past
belching smoke.

morning rush hour

with a lurch the train
shudders from the station
moving slowly at first
and then gaining speed
picks up the pace as trees
blur past the window to greet
my faded reflection.
directly across from me

a girl bites her lower lip
our knees bare inches away
from any chance at intimacy
and as she adjusts her i-phone
with white wireless earbuds
poking just beneath a woolen cap
the faintest notes
from some dance mix echoes
in the space between us.

her head slowly bobs with each beat
as the miles click metallically past
and i can't help but smile
at this distance awkwardly close
yet ages apart, isolated
as we are on different paths

which will never pass
so near again.

crack of dawn

gray skies &
wisps of smoke
climb in lazy circles

before
getting lost
in waves of cold air

stretching
miles above
slanted roofs and shuttered

rooms where
dreamless nights
eventually pass

until
it's time once
more to wear our masks.

number seven bus

the driver barely looks
as i pay the fare. all window
seats are taken.

most stare at phones
or have their heads buried
in a book.

the bus moves on
as i stagger up the aisle
anxious for a spot

while a woman
at the back knits patterns
from a ball of yarn.

mémère's trailer in laconia, nh

fronting the rusted trailer
long since abandoned the road
was more cart path than street
with hard-packed sand and stones and ruts
from car tires digging ever deeper
summer after summer after summer,
but june rains have transformed the lane
into a stream with rivulets
cascading down the hill
carrying small yellow leaves
and the occasional ant caught by surprise
while my tee shirt
soaked thru to the skin
clings to me tightly as i sit
on my heels and take it all in.

karmic wheel

another rusted sunset —
and underneath this rolling
wheel churning
day into day
and season into season

when there's nothing left to do
and nowhere left to run
and old familiar
escapes fall through
which no longer hold a reason,

and faced with faded memories
unrolled frame by frame
from its reel
or how the prophet told
that all returns into dust

or like chaff beneath the grinding
wheel or ash no longer fit
for flame and there's no one
left to blame —
just let it come undone.

a digression (really)

the first poem emerged while
sitting in the st louis university library
between classes.

it was usually cool and quiet
there and as an older student surrounded
by kids (really)

became a sort of refuge
from hormones and the oppressive
mid-september heat.

on fridays from the lobby's
windows you had a wonderful view of boys
toilet-papering

a row of maple tress across
the lane clearly many beers into another
lost weekend.

but who can blame them
since i was (really) no different when
serving overseas.

but i digress (something

i happen to be really good at, truth
be told). so, while

sitting on a second floor
sofa lost in thought with memories of her
words emerged

that seemed to me (really)
worth putting down on paper just to see
where they led.

and they led somewhere
sad and sweet and beautiful in seven
simple lines

about tears
rolling down her cheek.
(really).

night fall

she stared mysteriously
through me as the notes
of some sad sweet song
lingered along.
and like one who was lost
adrift or abandoned
i clung to each moment
afraid to move on,
bereft of a logic
or reasons.

she finally asked me to bed
and peeled back the covers
but i waited instead,
unsure of next moves
and stuck in my head
the moment came
and it went.
just another day's
energy spent.

for some love is a game
best played with a stranger
to use in the darkness
of an empty long night

without any thought
or a meaning,
driven by needs
and in search
of escape.

hung up (at the met)

they come by
in ones or twos
and sometimes in groups —
(a school field-trip
of uniformed children
laughing in line
or an adult painting
class with their earnest
instructor talking
about light and form
as gray-haired women
scribble notes) to pause
and pay homage
before some framed
canvas artfully hung
on display (but
the bulk simply run by
as if on a scavenger hunt
hurriedly snapping photos
from behind smart-phones
raised in front of faces
and often at bad angles
missing the finer details
and any possible point
altogether) and i wonder

what they feel
(or if most even bother
to have a single thought
at all) standing collectively
close and face to face
with another so-
called masterpiece.

starry night

beneath a tear-stained sky
the night cracked open wide
a million specks of light
can't dispel wandering thoughts
and adolescent dreams
for some reprieve
from this most uncivil
of places
unfit for living,
unmissed by grief.

heraclitus once wrote
how one can never step
into the same river twice
as the waters of life
continually change and flow,
a cosmic dance of space-time
with atoms constantly rearranged,
but if i could send
a single note back
against this inexorable tide
to my younger self
lying beneath that field of stars
and dreaming of peace
(or eternal release)

it might simply be this...
there's nothing
left to miss.

december dawn

gray skies and bitter cold
conspire to shut me indoors.

outside a few fluffy flakes
of snow
slightly heavier than air
float downwards

to dust unraked brown
leaves still scattered
across the empty acres
of my lawn.

county road 83

a ribbon of pavement
cuts through rolling fields

overgrown with thistle,
grasses and weeds.

turkey vultures glide in lazy
circles high above the street.

up ahead a derelict barn
decayed and abandoned

bakes in the sun, its faded
red planking consumed

by rot and long past
any need to replace.

and bolted to the peak
a rusted weather-vane

neglected for decades
is stuck facing east.

like filament

beneath a velveteen sky
hung with shadows and light
a jet streaks across the horizon
and flies till it's far out of sight
and i wonder how you might be feeling
as the day slips deep into dusk
while my dreams fragile as filament
melt in this westering sun
with thoughts spinning webs
out of nothing since it felt
like nothing was right.

below zero

bathed in early morning moonlight
a lone rabbit scuttles
over thin layers of crusty snow
blanketing my lawn
and pausing beneath an oak
nibbles at the few shoots of grass
able to poke through.

from behind thick panes of glass
i stand with coffee in hand
transfixed by the beat
of his tiny heart
until, with a start,
he's off scampering back
to his hole.

one moment

a half empty
cup of coffee
neglected
on my desk
slowly turns cold —

(while half
a world away)

a woman
in pink kimono
sits at attention,
and slightly
bent at her waist
pours
green tea.

ii. things

tin watering can

beside a rickety back step
painted pale gray

an old tin watering can
lays on its side

in an overgrown flower bed
now partly hidden

by weeds and a spray
of black-eyed susans.

sunflowers (ii)

cut and arranged.
stacked high on display
in a black earthenware vase.

a flower in a field
is still a wild thing beyond
the reach of any casual hand

(or passing glance)
but reduced to decoration
must find itself submitted

to the random rules
of grand design and left
to chance.

window ledge

painted figurines. a line
of rocks and crystals

arranged by size, shape
and alleged healing

properties. and hovering
just above stenciled

butterfly wings
her face once gazed

through double hung panes
out on a world

suffused in shades
of angst and wonder.

(for kayleen)

wedding photo

on the mantle,
a single photo
framed in faux silver.

a young couple
in shades of gray
stand stiffly

and smile through
the lens
of an opaque future.

from then until now
the slow roll
of years have eroded

moment by moment
any chance
of true communion

with roles
too easily filled
like an old pair of shoes.

dead leaves

dead leaves still matter
(even as we rake
them away to the compost
heap or stuff them deep
into plastic bags
readied for curbside pickup).

dead leaves matter
(even as their multi-colored shapes
decorate the lawn
while my neighbor mows
his into a fine mulch
shot from the discharge chute).

dead leaves might matter
more than we know
(or care to know as part
of a finely balanced ecosystem
on which so much
of our world depends).

or maybe they're just pretty.

gutter finds

rusted hubcap.
wire hanger.
ball of twine. three
soda cans, their tops
carefully removed
with a pair
of tin snips.

even gutter finds
can be redeemed
by hands
willing to get dirty
when viewed
through myth
and imagination

where all things
speak for themselves
(should you dare
to ask),
mirroring a reality
older than time
and drunk

on absinthe dreams

since nothing
is as it seems.
and there in a one room
apartment (more hovel
than home) trash
was transformed

into treasure
from the discarded remains
of our throw-
away society,
plucked from obscurity
and proudly left
on display.

(for asterios matakos, 1917 – 2002)

continental divide

while watching a youtube video my daughter
asked me about the "continental divide"
and what it might mean, what it "stands
for" (her words) and so i explained about
the imaginary line that runs from mountain
top to mountain top stretching from peak
to peak which divides the country in two.
and she said "oh, is that all?" yes, that's all.
it could have been named something else
or nothing at all. why divide a land by any
sort of lines and why name a mountain
one name and not another and who gets
to name it anyway? we live on "susan lane"
but only because the builder's daughter
was named susan, and so why not a street?
or a lane? and this town is called "newtown"
which is just another place to live in a "state"
called "connecticut" (by the way) and the list
could go on and on, name upon name
to identify and localize one particular place
from among many, which is useful for giving
or getting directions (i suppose) and helps
you navigate your way around this world.
but it's all too easy to forget that all lines
are imaginary as all names are arbitrary

and could easily be other than what they
happen to be, and that adding a name
to a place or fixing a label to the things
which comprise our collective space adds
nothing by way of value or meaning
and only seems to divide, by bisecting
things in two and separating "me"
from "you."

cans of soup

between deep thoughts and hyperbole
she asked me to stay
while the walls were littered
with pop art finds predominantly featuring
food stuffs and pantry items
divorced from reality and hung on display
as something other than avant-garde
to force a sort of paradigm shift —
or maybe just a new line of bullshit
to cover the simple fact
that our souls are fed on hunger
and drowning on junk food dreams
perpetually lost in a land
where nothing is as it seems.

(for andy warhol)

still life

beneath warm fleece sheets
she sleeps (dreaming of worlds
which could never
exist) and i can't resist
this inescapable urge
to ride those sweet
shallow waves of her breath
as deep as death
until i arrive
at the still beating heart
of eternity.

it's late. gently i peel
back the covers from our bed
to slip inside
and just when i rest my head
filled with nothing left
to lose and nothing
left to hide
she rolls instinctively
on her side.

sunflowers (iii)

in the grandest scheme
a flower is a flower
and nothing more
to be admired or consumed
or each in turn

(just as every summer
unwinds
its end season
into season to run
the perennial course,

and the tallest flowers
whither and bend
as fields of yellow
which once impressed
shrivel to brown

and then into dust)
yet i can't help thinking
as daylight fades
of what will become of us
now face to face

with primordial change

when there's nothing
left to trust.

manual typewriter

not the modern kind
but vintage, an antique
model with a black frame
and just the right
amount of rust
(some would
say "patina")
made by underwood.

each key punch sends
a thin arm flying upwards
which slaps against the drum
with a satisfying thud
(though the letter "g"
still feels a bit sticky
even after liberal
amounts of wd-40).

now a showpiece,
i imagine the woman
who could type sixty words
a minute on this machine
as her boss droned
mechanically along
about quarterly sales.

(sadly, by "boss"
i mean "man"

and by "woman"
i mean "secretary"),
because back in the day
that's how roles
used to play out
when conformity
was pre-ordained
and people were only
expected to know
their "place."

(for eleanor roosevelt)

a turnpike

so much once depended
on williams' red wheel
barrow
sitting beside chickens
ranging freely
across some farmer's
front lawn.

now a mini-mall graces
the landscape
with ubiquitous ease
hung with three
"for lease" signs
and fronted by state
route nineteen

while a line of cars
sit in traffic
belching smoke
as distracted drivers
check their texts
or listen to talk
radio.

blooming jasmine

a single drop of dew
heavy with the weight
of the world
hangs like a pearl
from a green fingertip of leaf.

i wade through
morning mist drunk from wine
and jasmine perfume
as rivulets of sweat
slide single-file

down the curve of my neck.
transfixed, i wait
suspended in time
as a single drop of dew
seems to hang

in midair milliseconds
before falling
to earth.

pearl earring

a slight turn of head.
her liquid gaze caught mid-
frame which sails past
all your defenses. face to face
with infinite shadow
and pale reflective surfaces
glazing over subterranean depths
suggestive of some hidden
motive or heart-felt desire
on the edge of a spoken word,
a mysterious train of thought
forever lost — hung and suspended
on her pursed red lips
like a pearl earring.

(for vermeer)

a locket

within an antique locket
hung with filigreed gold
a lock of his hair rests
safe and secure
held against all elements
and the shifting tides
of time as it rises
(or falls)
with each intake of breath
nestled so sweetly
against her breast.

sunflowers (iv)

i see them seemingly
everywhere i go and wonder
if they see me too.
at the grocery store
lined up in green plastic pots

near the sliding glass door
or by the chain link fence
in front of my daughter's school,
they stand up straight
(like i was taught to do)

and bask in warm summer
sunshine ever eager for more.
their big beautiful hearts
always seem open
and free (something

i was told never to be
about proverbial hearts
on proverbial sleeves)
forever facing the setting
sun. i see them seemingly
everywhere i go like an old
friend or a first date,

always the same and forever
new (and wonder if you
see them too).

(for theo & jo van gogh)

"So when one observes one's own life, and the life of the world in which we live, the daily monotonous, a life of routine, boredom, anxiety, fear, in that world is it possible to live a life that is free of fear, free of anxiety, a life that is a movement in which there is never a shadow of contradiction, therefore remorse and the invitation to all kinds of violence and self-centered activity?"

– J Krishnamurti

Acknowledgments

Life is a journey. Or pilgrimage. But rather than walking a path to some fabled shrine in a distant land, we're (hopefully) on the journey of self-discovery, of bravely plumbing those subterranean depths which typically only emerge in dreams.

And like every journey there are many fellow travelers we meet along the way. Some only share a few short moments of their life with us before venturing off toward other horizons, while others become fellow traveling companions walking alongside for long stretches of time.

In my life I've been blessed with many people who have aided me along this journey and who have shown me such tender care and loving kindness during our time together. To all of you (and you know who you are) this page is addressed as my humble and heartfelt thank you.

Cover artwork by Osnat Tzadok, www.osnatfineart.com
Cover design by Angie @ pro_ebookcovers

About Michael R Guerin

Michael R. Guerin is a veteran of the U.S. Air Force, a former Catholic religious community postulant and the founder of Success Marketing, a web design firm. He has a Master's Degree in Philosophy from Fordham University, is the author of eight books of poetry (available on amazon.com), a Lenormand Deck & Guidebook and the creator of a van Gogh inspired oracle deck (available on etsy.com).

Since 2008 he has set up, redesigned or fixed more than six hundred websites, many for holistic health practitioners. He recently completed his first novel, THE OTHERSIDE, which is the first of a planned four book series titled "The Wanderer." The series is a past-life recollection which weaves together four different historical timelines and focuses on love, loss, mission and redemption. He currently lives in St. Petersburg, Florida with his wife and family.